# Quotidian Poems
# by Arnold David Richards

# Quotidian Poems

### Arnold David Richards

International Psychoanalytic Books
New York • http://www.IPBooks.net

**Quotidian Poems**

Published by IPBooks, Queens, NY
Online at IPBooks.net

Cover Picture: Liubov Popova, *Painterly Architectonic (Still Life: Instruments)* 1915, Russia.
Cover layout by Kathy Kovacic, Blackthorn Studio.
Interior design and layout by Noel S. Morado.

ISBN: 978-1-956864-92-2

# Contents

Preface by Merle Heidi Molofsky ..................................... 1

Boss: A Meditation ................................. 9

Arlene ................................................. 11

Friends ................................................ 12

Father's Day ......................................... 13

Mother's Day 1 ...................................... 15

Petersburg, VA, 1965 .............................. 17

For My Much Younger Sister on the Occasion
of Her Birthday ..................................... 18

Elegy for Muriel ..................................... 20

Borough Park ........................................ 21

A Requiem ............................................ 24

Mother's Day 2 ...................................... 25

Button .................................................. 26

Poetry is Memoir: My Father's Unhappy Life ................... 28

Today March 11 Was My Sister's Birthday ..................... 30

Poem in Progress .................................... 31

Rhyme or Reason .................................... 33

Meaning ................................................ 34

Scissors and Paste ................................... 35

Poetry Celebrates the Ordinary .................... 36

Poetry .................................................. 38

Treasure ............................................... 39

Poetry is a Commentary on Life ................... 40

Musings ................................................ 41

T.S. Eliot Reads: The Love Song of J. Alfred Prufrock ......42

Language .................................................................44

A Love Affair ...........................................................45

Poetry ....................................................................46

Poetry is Economy .....................................................47

Internet ..................................................................48

Hayden Planetarium ...................................................49

Physics ...................................................................51

Pi ..........................................................................53

Space Travel ............................................................54

Dark Matter .............................................................55

Quantum Entanglement ...............................................56

The Uncertainty Principle ............................................58

Quantum Mechanics ...................................................60

Quantum Entanglement 2 .............................................61

Black Holes .............................................................62

Scientists ................................................................63

Expansion ...............................................................64

We Are Alone ...........................................................65

Extinction ...............................................................66

Poincaré .................................................................67

The End is Near ........................................................68

Life .......................................................................69

Coda ......................................................................70

90 ..........................................................................71

There Are So Many I Miss ............................................73

Time ......................................................................74

As We Grow Older .....................................................75

Retirement ..............................................................76

How Does It Feel? ......................................................77

Getting Old ............................................................78
Dominion................................................................79
Bereft ....................................................................80
Addendum ............................................................81
Wreath of Verses ...................................................82
Study Group ..........................................................85
Summertime...........................................................86
Equinox .................................................................88
Death ....................................................................89
Eye .......................................................................90
A Picture at The Prado ...........................................91
Turtle ....................................................................93
On The Run ..........................................................94
Synagogue .............................................................95
The Talmud............................................................96
Dreams..................................................................97
Memory: My Life ....................................................98
Anniversary Song....................................................100

# Preface

The poems in *Quotidian*, a superb collection of poetry by Arnold Richards, exemplify a profound theme, Poetry is Memoir, and indeed it is! These poems tell the story of Arnold Richards' life, beginning with events in his family's life before his parents even met, before he was born, to his childhood in Borough Park, Brooklyn, New York, and continuing through the many decades until the time the book was published, when he was 90 years old.

The book begins with "Boss: A Meditation, A Hasidic Parable", an excerpt from *Gates of the Forest* by Elie Wiesel, in which Elie Wiesel indeed recounts a deeply meaningful Hasidic parable about what we remember concerning tradition and the Jewish relationship with God. The parable concludes with a marvelous tribute to story-telling: "God made man because he loves stories".

If we are made in the image of the Creator, in the image of God, then we certainly will recognize and acknowledge that we too love stories. Children often ask, "Tell me a story". And an adult in touch with one's inner child also will want to ask, "Tell me a story".

We are fortunate that we can read this memoir in poetry, and if others reading are like me, then we all can love, and resonate with, Arnie's stories. Arnie's commentary on God making man because he loves stories, is "Boss laughs". Our vital experiences, our deeply felt memories, are reduced to a story that we all have heard before, a Yiddish saying, "Mann tracht und Gott lacht", "Mankind plans, and God laughs". The Boss laughs at our hopes and dreams. Arnold Richards is a well-known Yiddishist. I am sure that he would also appreciate the Scots version, exemplified by a fellow poet, Robert Burns, 18th century CE, who wrote, "The best-laid schemes of mice and men gang aft agley", usually rephrased in contemporary English as "The best-laid plans of mice and men oft go astray".

The title of this collection is Quotidian. The word means ordinary, every day. There is nothing "ordinary" about this engrossing poetic memoir. Actually, this collection is extraordinary. Arnie finds the sparkling jewel, the radiant light, in the "ordinary", in "every day" life.

This collection is organized into groupings, into themes. There are poems about Arnie's family, about Arnie's childhood, about poetry itself, about language, about science, poems that are elegies, poems that are tributes. Arnie is a noted psychoanalyst, and thus, we can assume that his poetic musings are psychoanalytically informed, that Psyche may be his Muse.

A key element in both poetry and psychoanalysis is symbolism. His poems about science, which also includes technology, have evocative titles, such as "Internet", "Hayden Planetarium", "Physics", "Pi", "Time", "Space Travel", "Dark Matter", "Quantum Entanglement", "The Uncertainty Principle", "Quantum Mechanics", "Quantum Entanglement", "Black Holes". He imbues his exploration of complex scientific concepts with an appreciation of the underlying symbolism, an acknowledgment of the romance of science.

In "Hayden Planetarium", he considers a major concept about the origin of the universe, the Big Bang theory, and reminds us to remember a famous poem by T.S. Eliot, "The Hollow Men", with the memorable lines, "This is the way the world ends/ not with a bang but a whimper". Arnie amplifies the sounds of the world ending, with his lines, "In burp or blast/ Or whimper". As we take note of the burp, we then are treated to the romance of the universe, the embodiment of love and death as gods in ancient Greece, Eros and Thanatos, names that Sigmund Freud used in developing psychoanalytic theory to represent what he considered the life drive and the death drive. Arnie brings his poetic sensibility, his imagination, his awareness of symbolism, and his scientific knowledge of critical mass, to conceive of a universe in which we find "Eros and Thanatos/ Frozen in a final/ Embrace".

In "Pi", as he contemplates the infinite decimals that comprise the ratio of pi, he considers the limitations death puts on human life, noting that "we have to leave/ at a finite time". Thus, the mathematical reality does not comfort us in our thwarted yearning for eternal life.

His poems that address language, meaning, and poetry capture the sublime in human existence. Yes, the sublime is part of quotidian experience! In "Language", he alerts us to recognizing that human history is the history of human language. In "Poetry", he begins by saying that 'each one of us has a poetic voice/ unique and special/ it describes experience/ in our own language/ rooted in our past". This is an affirmation of the constant presence of the availability of poetry and meaning in language, imbued with psychoanalytic insight, that our past is always present in our every day. In "Language", he mystifies us by telling us that language is a mystery, and then surprises us at the end of the poem by taking us to the Sumeria of 40,000 years ago.

Of course he surprises us! In his poem "Rhyme or Reason", in which he considers whether to explore poetry or stick with science, he concludes by saying, "and apples fall/ like planets/ said Newton/ but I like/ Surprises!"

In a number of his poems, Arnie enters into dialogue with other poets. His engagement with other poets brings to mind the 1973 book by literary critic Harold Bloom, *The Anxiety of Influence*. Yet, it seems to me Arnie is not afflicted with the anxiety of influence, but, rather, he enjoys commonality and differentiation. He responds to T.S. Eliot's "Love Song of J. Alfred Prufrock" by affirming that "I also grow old/ but I won't wear the bottom/ of my trousers rolled".

In "Eye", Arnie asks, "can an eye/ make itself", and ends, "or only God/ can make an eye/ so we can see". He is acknowledging the poem "Trees", by Joyce Kilmer, who says, "I think that I shall never see/ A poem lovely as a tree". I find no need to ponder if a poem can be as lovely as a tree, or to compare poems with the loveliness of nature. I will celebrate Arnie's observation that God made an eye so we can see. And, perhaps, however Arnie came to be the poet he is, I will delight in the poems he has written and that he shares with us.

In "How Does It Feel", an aging Arnold Richards encounters the once 23-year-old Bob Dylan, who, in 1965, wrote "Like a Rolling Stone", and asked, "How does it feel?". Arnie replies, "not like a complete unknown/ like a rolling stone".

In "Dominion", Arnie challenges Dylan Thomas, who averred, "And death shall have no dominion". Arnie, who has mourned the deaths of so many, declares, "death does have dominion/ too many departed to feel fully alive".

Arnie has two sections in *Quotidian* that are devoted to elegies, to requiems, to mourning the deaths of family members and of friends and colleagues. Yes, they are moving, and beautifully written.

Yet he also affirms life. He affirms life, and love. He may write a poem in which he envisions Eros and Thanatos locked in a frozen embrace, but, when he loves fully, and indeed he does, he affirms Eros.

To fully appreciate poetry as memoir, we have to enter into Arnie's world, beginning with a long-unfolding "now", a love affair, with his poem to his wife, "Arlene", aglow with saying, "You are my wife/ and you are my life/ and you are my love/ and you are my treasure". This is a remarkable, lovely tribute to 71 years of marriage. They indeed are each other's love.

In a later poem, "90", he concludes, "we write new/ and love chapters/ love love/ ever more".

Then, we segue to memories of his childhood and his family. He begins with honoring his father and mother, with "Father's Day", and then "Mother's Day 1". We tremble as we learn of Arnie's father's troubled childhood, then his maturing and reaching old age, and then his shocking, violent death. This violent death is a traumatic, defining moment for Arnie. We understand how much he loved and will always love his father, and how he must confront the reality. "Mother's Day 1" is a loving description of what brought every day joy to his mother, her simple quotidian pleasures. "For My Much Younger Sister on the Occasion of Her Birthday" is a loving tribute, and an acknowledgment of benign sibling rivalry. He wonders, "Who cut our ties at birth?", and admits, "I am our father's son/ You are our mother's child".

In "Borough Park", Arnie again mourns his father, his father's violent death. He cites a "headline in *The Forward*" (a Jewish newspaper), "CRIPPLE STABBED IN BORO PARK". What a wrenching line to put in a poem. What a wrenching line to read. How wrenching life can be! He cites everything his father survived in Europe and the Middle East before coming to the United States, for instance, as a member of Trotsky's army, in fighting the Ukrainian army, bandits, Arabs in Galilee, only to be murdered in a robbery in Borough Park, Brooklyn.

Other poems concerning family do give us a glimpse into the quotidian. "Mother's Day 2", with mother's and children's lives a tapestry, woven together. "Button", describing his extended family's involvement in manufacturing buttons, particularly during World War II.

We encounter the poignancy of "Poetry is Memoir: My Father's Unhappy Life". Arnie, the poet son of a long-suffering, disappointed, murdered man, recounts details, and then realizes, "I gave him pleasure/ three grandchildren/ I went to medical school/ I became a doctor/ he did not have a happy life/ no pleasures or satisfaction/ I gave him pleasure and satisfaction/ I like to think".

In reading this book of every day ordinary extraordinary experience, we gain insight into what truly matters, what a poet/ scientist/psychoanalyst/son/father/husband/human being tells us about life, life and death, memories, discoveries....

Arnie offers us so much in "Poetry is a Commentary on Life", beginning with "on the sublime and the banal/ the ordinary and the extraordinary", and concluding with "poetry makes life worth living/ living makes poetry worth writing".

In "Life", Arnie offers a delightful possibility, a possibility offered by creativity: "Fly on the wings of your imagination/ soaring birds".

In this book of poetry, we can enjoy flying on the wings of imagination, through language, science, memories, contemplating life and death, symbolism, the playful freedom of meaning, ideas, and discovery, the extraordinary ordinary quotidian every day.

Merle Heidi Molofsky

# Boss: A Meditation
### A Hasidic Parable

When the great Rabbi Israel Baal Shem-Tov saw misfortune threatening the Jews it was his custom to go into a certain part of the forest to meditate. There he would light a fire, say a special prayer, and the miracle would be accomplished and the misfortune averted.

Later, when his disciple, the celebrated Magid of Mezritch, had occasion, for the same reason, to intercede with heaven, he would go to the same place in the forest and say: "Master of the Universe, listen! I do not know how to light the fire, but I am still able to say the prayer," and again the miracle would be accomplished.

Still later, Rabbi Moshe-Leib of Sasov, in order to save his people once more, would go into the forest and say: "I do not know how to light the fire, I do not know the prayer, but I know the place and this must be sufficient." It was sufficient and the miracle was accomplished.

Then it fell to Rabbi Israel of Rizhyn to overcome misfortune. Sitting in his armchair, his head in his hands, he spoke to God: "I am unable to light the fire and I do not know the prayer; I cannot even find the place in the forest. All I can do is to tell the story, and this must be sufficient." And it was sufficient.

God made man because he loves stories.

— Elie Wiesel, *The Gates of the Forest*

The largest structure in the universe
838 separate galaxies
One billion light years across
Four connected clusters
How many moons planets ?
People like us
We start the day
Infinite worlds
Inconceivable
All the concerns of our
Life seem reasonable
We think
Boss laughs
Inconsequential
And us
Infinitesimal

# Arlene

you are my wife
and you are my life
you are my love
you are my treasure
the fount of my pleasure
you connect
with the depth of my being
life worth living
beginning without ending
always connected
and connecting
we are a double helix
intertwined
you and me
you grace the hours
and all our days

# Friends

friends for ever and ever
always for the better
caring and sharing
a life time of memories
indelible
now and then
and always

# Father's Day

My father had a stubble beard
a crippled gait, a sad face, a quiet voice

My father had a troubled life.
Mother died before her time.
Brother struck by Cossack blade.
Father carried the body home.
Sister shot in dark ravine.
A world destroyed, A god that failed..

My father grew old. His hair turned white.
A wrinkled suit wrapped his frame,

He walked home.
Stooped, returned to wife
Bandit waited in darkened hall

Blood unstopped stained the wall.

My father had a troubled life,
a crippled gait, a stubble beard
a sad face, a quiet voice

A troubled life
And then he died.

# Mother's Day 1

My mother was
a Hallmark junkie.
Collected cards
Dates received
recorded in her book
pages wide-ruled
black-and-white
speckled cover
the gift noted
where applicable
House plant:
"It lasts but it needs
watering"
Flowers by telegraph:
"A visit would
have been better"
A thimble to add
to her collection.

She hung the cards
on a line strung
across the rough stone
basement wall
white powdered surface
sheets out to dry
printed wishes
flower-bordered
rhymed couplets
written by
the poet laureates
of Kansas City.

# Petersburg, VA, 1965

I was the jailer
You were the jailed

We plotted your escape.
Dark night at Southern Depot.
First stop on the underground railway
Route to freedom.

No more chain gang dogs Greyhound
route to freedom.

Missed by a minute or less
Sinking heart, sweaty palms
Who decided you or I Impala
Route to freedom

No more nigger work wife I 95
Route to freedom.

# For My Much Younger Sister on the Occasion of Her Birthday

Shall I mark your birthday when you did not mark mine?

We both started in same space but at the wrong time.
I too soon.  You too late.
You  Sarah's gift.. I a mistake

Down the same canal. Greeted by the same face
Brought to the same place.
Crowded and cluttered rooms with little view.
Windows covered with damask opaque to leaves and sky
Furniture covered with plastic.
Transparent in pattern shielding texture from the feel of sticky
fingers
yours and mine.

We both ate In the same kitchen. Sanitas on the walls,
linoleum on the floor
Fox's U-Bet Chocolate Syrup, My*T*Fine Chocolate Pudding

We shared space and place faced but not time.
I came to love the man who also made us both.
You were taught otherwise.

Who cut our ties of birth?
I am our father's son.
You are our mother's child.

# Elegy for Muriel

You celebrated your self
and rightly so.
You reveled in your senses,
pampered them with aliment
sonatas and sauces
flavorful.
You tuned your body
Sharpened its sensuality
prepared for its adornment,
clothes your advertisement.
You wrote your own
jacket copy
prideful
before your
fall.

Muriel Weinstein, PhD died two summers ago. She fell off a
mountain in Switzerland where she loved to climb,

# Borough Park

Color it red
If you don't mind
I will call
a spade a spade
was it a buck knife
or switch blade impaled the painter' s chest wall
red blood spurting
on tiled floor
of dark hallway
headline in *The Forward*
CRIPPLE STABBED IN BORO PARK
red blood like spray paint
my father's last job
price complete
includes labor and materials,

He always lived dangerously
soldier-librarian
in Trotsky's army
he escaped bandits
and commissars
British shells
crashing on Odessa
Romanian border guards

Arabs In Galilee
He came to America
land of promise
He died the day after
the Fourth of July
red white and blue
celebration of
our revolution
ironic, ex-Bolshevik
killed by worker
dead like brother
bayonetted by Petliura

He should have stuck to books
or stayed
a worker, Mottle
the boss not the
operator. Or kept
the payroll In the bank,
skipped the evening news
and advertised in the
Yellow Pages:
Workmen's compensation
fully covered
estimates cheerfully given
windows for eight dollars
fire escapes for twenty-five

Benjamin Moore paint the best
but don't forget
Dutch Boy red lead
undercoat first
if you don't mind.

# A Requiem

there are so many I miss
so many are gone
a requiem for a world friends my father watched for me and  the
family
all at rest blessed I'm sure,
but not here for me.
My words fall on no one's ears.
My smile is invisible.
 My laughter is inaudible. They are ghost ephemeral
Not material but present in memory
and all of the life that we live together
together indelible
etched marked
written and  preserved
I am here the past
Worlds and people to be enjoyed
savored like a succulent
fruit cherished,
like an icon celebrated
like a victory now

# Mother's Day 2

Your day is your
children's day
and your children's day
Is our day
Seamless
Our lives intertwined
Without interruption
A tapestry
Life on a loom
Woven
Together

# Button

I grew up in a button family
pearl buttons
not plastic
for made to order custom shirts
for the affluent
my uncle joe
western button company
on west 26 street
my uncle Irving
Arrow Button Company
1199 Broadway
on the fifth floor
508
I went there every Saturday
on the west end
BMT
I packed cases
for shipping
the steel stretcher
my job
my uncle watched
then lunch at the automat
a quarter for
an egg salad sandwich

ten cents for an orange drink
and then the West End BMT
ride home
my mother sorted buttons
her fingers flew
selecting the buttons according to grade
good better best
I watched
and my mother got paid
we needed money it was war time
my father painted liberty ships
left early and came back late
federal shipbuilding and dry dock company
a division of US Steel

# Poetry is Memoir:
# My Father's Unhappy Life

fathers mother died when he was 13
his brothers was murdered by Pitliura
he graduated by correspondence
from the gymnasium
the only Jew from his town
he started a middle school with his sister
when he was 15
he should have gone to university
but the revolution came
1917
librarian in Trotsky's army
he drove the cart
with the books
got typhus
hospitalized in Odessa
the British shelled the city
befriended by a Jewish medical couple
he would go to medical school
his father said no
deserted the army
crossed over to Rumania
sailed from Brindizi

to Alexandria
to Haifa
to Nahalal
to Montreal
to Brooklyn
he was a scholar
who became a house painter
not a professor
few pleasures
few satisfactions
he didn't travel
he didn't eat in restaurants
he didn't succeed in business
my mother was happier
she had two sisters
two brothers nearby
he had two brothers
far away
the Soviet Union
and Brazil
last seen in 1920
i gave him pleasure
three grandchildren
I went to medical school
I became a doctor
he did not have a happy life
no pleasures or satisfaction
I gave him pleasure and satisfaction
I like to think

# Today March 11 Was My Sister's Birthday

she knew me longer than anyone else
when she was alive
we had years of memories together
our parents lived in our minds
eighteen months apart
not a long time
we were close
we should have been rivals
but we weren't
she celebrated my achievements
it was simple
she loved me
and I loved her
up and down
and now she's gone

# Poem in Progress

My poems
are personal
forged
in the oven
of my discontent
tempered by the fire
of my passion
which burns words
on white paper
like an electric tool
marks wood

and smoke
into the nostrils
perfumes
the page
on which I
the artisan
sets down
my lusts
and rage.

But art abhors
the confessional.
I will use artifice
to engage
my audience,
disguise to veil
the obvious,
guile to create
illusion
as I ply my trade.

# Rhyme or Reason

I write a
poem search
for rhyme
and rule
but line
falls flat
I juggle
words
In desperation

Should I stick
to science?
Galileo said
the laws of
shadow making
are the same
on the moon
as on the earth
and apples fall
like planets
said Newton
But I like
Surprises

# Meaning

meaning matters
wonder of wonder
how does a caterpillar become a butterfly
evolution
or design
how does a sparrow learn to fly
how does a whale learn to dive
how does the summer become the fall
how will the world survive
if the glaciers melt
and the corals die
who is in charge
are we masters of our fate
the clock ticks
the sun sets
and the music stops

# Scissors and Paste

Poetry
Cuts up life
Into pieces
And pastes them
On a page

# Poetry Celebrates the Ordinary

people, places and things,
events and happenings
The words of the poem are the lyrics of the poet's song
a song  to be sung and resung
the libretto  of the opera
MonteVerdi in Milan
Wagner in Vienna, Bayreuth, and Salzburg
Mussorgsky in Moscow

poetry is ostentatious
Poetry is presumptuous
our sensibility
our humanity
our creativity
our eternity
A poem a day is better than an apple
comic
Surprise
End of the poet's song

A poem is like the lyric of a song or the libretto of an opera. The poet provides the words and the listener hears the music. It is a creative collaboration, which touches the humanity of each of us. The symphony of the gods, the music of the soul.

# Poetry

is economy
compression
of thoughts and feelings
attention to meaning
multiple connotations
language direct
and embellished
simile and metaphor
phrases turned
lessons learned
the highest art form
Virgil
the poet of poets
for the ages
cummings sang of Olaf

# Treasure

treasure every measure
treasure every pleasure
poetic license
the best is yet to come
gratification
satisfaction
we move between fantasy and reality
to  our benefit
the world is our playground
we ride our teeter totter
up down
up down
a measure of pleasure
and joy

# Poetry is a Commentary on Life

on the sublime and the banal
the ordinary and the extraordinary
the words of poetry
underline meaning and emotion
help us decide what is important
what is not
what makes life worth living
what is inconsequential
what matters
etched on an anvil
words have prominence
and permanence
for all to listen
for all to hear
others
and our self
and ultimately
our posterity
poetry makes life worth living
living makes poetry worth writing

# Musings

I write about the human condition
how we live
and when we die
who we are
and who we hope to be
I write about pleasure and pain
about our losses
and about our gains
trauma and tragedy
triumph and ecstasy
our life is a mosaic
or a tapestry
woven threads
a mystery
but meaningful
preserved in memory
for us
and all

# T.S. Eliot Reads: The Love Song of J. Alfred Prufrock

time time
for you and me
quotidian
ordinary stuff
for you and me
does it matter
who I am
what I do
no matter
an instant
or eternity
for ever
or never
now or then
past or future
spring or all
you and me
or others
creating
or destroying
hoping
yearning

resigned
it is what it is
it is what will be
big things
and small stuff
spring or fall
summer winter
rain or shine
sun and
clouds
seasons
reasons
I also grow old
but I won't wear the bottom
of my trousers rolled

# Language

language is a mystery
a human necessity
meaning comes from the order of the words
Cain killed Abel
Abel killed Cain
the difference matters
where am I going
a place
I am going to eat a steak
a purpose
what is going on
a happening
going
gone
it started in Sumeria
40000 years ago

# A Love Affair

poetry
is brevity
and brevity
is the spice of wit
less is more
economy of words
the poet communicates with his audience
the audience celebrates the poet
a love affair
for ever

# Poetry

each one of us has
a poetic voice
unique and special
it describes experience
in our own language
rooted in our past
and present
conscious
and unconscious
we have a poem maker
at work night and day
awake and asleep
deposits words on a blank sheet of paper
for all to read
and remember

# Poetry is Economy

words, and feelings
Expressed succinctly
convey to many
What we think and feel
if man can move mountains
people can move hearts and minds
We were born to make a difference
Our obligation
our responsibility
A challenge to fulfill

# Internet

betwixt and between
takes up our time
and the space
between us and then
more text
less feeling
humanity
on hold
mindless

# Hayden Planetarium

Color it dark matter
Dispersed exactly
In the universe
The cosmos poised
Precariously at conception
On a teeter totter

Density is destiny
Miscount six atoms
Per square meter
And the Big Bang ends
In burp or blast
Or whimper

Mass is critical
Cold dark matter
Even if invisible
Gathers up the galaxies
Like love the great
Attractor

Color it dark
Like death
Eros and Thanatos
Frozen in a final
Embrace

# Physics

Born and Bohr
quantum physics and more
Heisenberg
complementarity
we can't know
everything at
once
we defer to our maker
who shakes our
world
questions
and no answers
wave or particle
or vibrating strings
Pauli's principle
Planck's constant
fixed
immutable

Einstein
and God
comes up
snake eyes
rolling
rolling
on the river of
life
end of my song

# Pi

can not be expressed
as the ratio of two integers
it is a decimal representation
that never ends.
our maker has made the universe
continue to infinity
but we have to leave
at a finite time

# Space Travel

our ordinary life is earthbound
and hidebound
but for some this is not acceptable
we strive for transcendence
offered by space travel
exploration
of the universe
every achievement
moon planet
and beyond
is celebrated
marked in our calendar
date and time
the astronauts
fly for all of us
and achieve special recognition
in the log
of our humanity

# Dark Matter

ordinary matter the stuff of galaxies
and stars is only one sixth of the stuff that exits in our universe
the rest is dark matter which we know is there but can't find
first there was the WIMP
interacting with the universe through gravity
part of the theory of
supersymmetry
but the search always came up short
then there were AXIONS named
after a box of laundry detergent
colorful
the goal is how to catch one
super colliders
monstrous magnets
in the laboratory
or in outer space
the jury is still out and
the universe is still open

dark matter
no matter

# Quantum Entanglement

Einstein called quantum entanglement "spooky action at a
distance"
he said he found it hard to believe
even though he made it up
with Podolsky and Rosen
EPR
Schrödinger anticipated this
and wrote the definitive paper
how can one proton know what the other is doing at a great
distance
toss two coins
they both come up heads
or tails
one coin knows
what the other is doing
not the way we think
the quantum world
is profoundly different
from our ordinary world

reality has a new dimension
entanglement is not reasonable
but is necessary
Einstein in the end
accepted his spooky world
and a higher power

# The Uncertainty Principle

the uncertainty principle of Heisenberg
is a foundational concept in modern physics
it states that there is a limit
to what can be known about the physical world
about small entities
like atoms electrons and photons
it states that it is not possible
to determine precisely
the mass and the momentum
of an individual particle,
the act of measuring limits
our ability to establish precisely mass and momentum
it violated our need for a determinative universe
a universe that can be known to each one of us
Einstein disagreed with Heisenberg
Bohr agreed

Bohn wrote a letter to Heisenberg
which he didn't send
there was concern that Heisenberg would help Hitler
build an atom bomb
because he remained in Germany
but he insisted he would not
and most believed him
I know what I know
and I see what I see
I am certain

# Quantum Mechanics

quantum mechanics deals with probabilities
Pauli had his principle
Planck had his constant
Planck published papers
Pauli wrote letters
the Pauli principle stated that two fermions with opposite spins
could not occupy the same place at the same time
Planck's constant states that the energy of a photon is equal to
its frequency multiplied by Planck's constant  and the wavelength
of a matter wave
is equal to its frequency divided by its particle momentum
it predicts the distribution of thermal radiation from a closed
furnace black body radiation
Planck called this the constant of action
central to Einstein's theory of relativity
the first Solvay conference in 1911 was devoted to the theory
of radiation and quanta
quantum mechanics is our window on the divine
our view of the fabric of the universe
probabilistic
but definable

# Quantum Entanglement 2

four worlds defy our imagination and understanding
quantum entanglement
challenges our view of reality
but it all can be recovered with a kiss

# Black Holes

black holes are universal
in our universe
every galaxy has one

matter can not escape
stuck in space
gravitational waves
trapped

defies our understanding
predicted by Einstein's theory of relativity
does it affect our lives
we think not
what is the message
makes us humble
minor players
in an awesome world

# Scientists

Newton replaced Descartes
Einstein replaced Newton
Feynman replaced Einstein
each stood on the shoulders of the other.
Is there a limit to what we can know? Maybe

# Expansion

faster faster
the universe is expanding
dark energy
dark matter
both matter
Hubble Constant number
not a whimper
a big bang
positrons
flee from each other
faster faster

# We Are Alone

are we alone?
a singularity
no other life in space
or are we one of many
many many planets in the universe
life on many others
dark energy makes it happen
and our specialness is undone
is that acceptable?
probably not
we are not the center of the universe
and not the only one living in the universe
the ultimate
narcissistic blow

# Extinction

who will replace us when we are gone
the octopus we are told
eight limbs
and a big head
a computer like brain
energy from the tides
tidal power
will live in the ocean
they will multiply
communicate
socialize
calculate
our successors
will survive

# Poincaré

Poincaré said
the answer is philosophy
philosophy is meaning not feeling
what is the question?

who am I?
do you believe in free will
of course I do, Mr. Singer said
I have no choice

who am I?
geography Boro Park
ethnicity the Tribe
ideology the God that failed
first my first name for $50
then my second name

who am I?
I will make myself
I will forge myself in the smithy
of my soul

# The End is Near

The end is near
a black hole approaches
arrives in 200 years
life is finite
time is limited
we do not have
a privileged place in the universe
ephemeral
hurling to
our demise
period
or punctuation mark?

at the end
of time

# Life

squeeze what you can
out of every moment
treasure every pleasure
enjoy every joy
go down to the sea
lie in the water
come in with the tide
fly on the wings of your imagination
soaring birds

# Coda

I have had a long life
a happy life
a satisfied life
a productive life
connecting with many
overcoming traumas
an upward trajectory
pleasing
and being pleased
more than I hoped for
more than I ever expected
I will continue
until the clock stops
and the light goes out
I will leave my memoir
and my legacy
for all

# 90

at age 90 I look back
and I look forward
looking back
I am aware of a lifetime of experience
connections
relationships
accomplishments
roads taken
roads not taken
no way of knowing the outcome
of roads we did not pursue
but no matter
we arrived where
we arrived
and we are here
ready to go on
the next ten years are our own
but they are profoundly affected

by the last 90
opportunity for new connections
for new creations
we write new chapters
and love
love love
ever more

# There Are So Many I Miss

so many are gone
requiem for a world, friends
my father watched  over me and  the family
all at rest blessed I'm sure, but not here for me.
My words fall on no ears
My smile is invisible. My laughter is in audible.
They are ghost femoral not
material but present in memory
and all of the life that we live together
together
indelible etched marked written and
preserved
i am here the past
world and people to be enjoyed savored like a succulent,
fruit cherished, like an icon
celebrated like a victory now

# Time

is inexorable
every period has a beginning
and a middle and an end
until the final curtain
falls for all
time shows no mercy
or compassion
the world doesn't stop
but we have to get off
and join all other departed
what did Woody Allen say?
I am not afraid of death
I just don't want to be there when it happens

# As We Grow Older

as we grow older
we remember our younger years
the games we played
the food we ate
the songs we sang
hopscotch jump rope double dutch
handball stick ball punch ball touch tackle court
court ringolevio
johnny on the pony
poker bridge chess checkers water polo
the food
We ate charlotte russe licorice popsicle,
creamsicle, fudgsicle, halvah, malted milk,
egg cream, black and white soda,
songs of protest
we shall overcome
blowing in the wind
and anarchist's garret
factory windows are always broken
and of the factory windows
song and end of my song

# Retirement

retirement is
when things that once
mattered
no longer matter
been everywhere
done everything
no more getting
and spending
the day divided
into breakfast
lunch and supper
let the world come to you
you don't have to meet the world
unless you want to
you become invulnerable
nothing is unbearable
waking and sleeping
becomes your rhythm
dreams a source of excitement
but what you see
is only a dream
the curtain closes
and the next day begins

# How Does It Feel?

to be where you always wanted to be
how does it feel
to have accomplished all that you wanted to get done
how does it feel
to be at the top of your game
how does it feel
not like a complete unknown
like a rolling stone

# Getting Old

90 is a strange time
time is no longer infinite
and it's hard to understand why not
I just cycled 3 miles on my tricycle
I didn't huff or puff
I felt fine
and thought I could go another 3 miles
who is ending my run
and why
the grand plan is puzzling
don't stop the world
I don't want to get off
I want to remain forever
immortality is a wish
that Freud did not recognize
but I believe it's universal
experienced by all
as we rage rage rage
against the dying of the light
but I feel fine
my maker needs a new plan
eternity for me
and for all

# Dominion

many recent and
many long ago memories
fill every day
we dream about the dead at night
and some are alive in the dream
fulfilling our wishes
and disappointing when we awake
is this all part of a cosmic plan
which we don't understand
we can't escape our mortality
death does have dominion
too many departed
to feel fully alive

# Bereft

seven close friends died this year
Ernie Sandy Marty Mike Leon Albert Chuck
mostly younger
frequent conversations
important connections
social interactions
**bereft**

# Addendum

Ernie Kafka Sandy Abend Mike Porter Al Sax Leon Balter Chuck
Rothstein Marty Willick

all gone
we miss them very much
they can't hear us
they can't see us
we mourn their loss
but we celebrate our existence
like eating a succulent fruit
or a ripe peach
and listen to the dolphins
singing each to each other
until the lights go out
and the clock stops
for all of us

# Wreath of Verses
## (On the Fresh Grave of Toni Greenberg)

Color it black
If you don' t mind
Her eyes shut tight
"Shakhor b'eynatim"
Black decorates our hall
Our no longer happy
Birthday Party and hers
Danzig/Vilna 1925
God would not delay
Her departure for our
Benefit

Color it black
Color of mourning
Darkens our vision
"Tunkl in di oygn"
She carried history
On her person
Khasidik Queen
Superordinate to Kaiser

And Emperor
God would not delay
Her departure for our
Purpose

Color it black
If you don't mind
Her eyes shut tight
"Khoyshekh b'eynayim"
Curtain falls
On Central Park window
Dusk drops early in December
But it was a warm autumn
Did God delay winter
This year to ease her exit?

Color it black
Funereal
Yankele, Toni's emissary
And God's messenger
Followed her instructions
To the letter
Stamped with date/time

Like a computer
She summoned the players
For the final performance
She was a star .
She had the right
To schedule closing night
For her benefit
"Finster in di oygn"
Color it darkness

# Study Group

Freud asked what do
women want Not so wise
a man I thought maybe
he didn't know everything

My students are women groupies
hang on every word and I tell
good jokes besides they think
I know everything.

I dazzle with my erudition\ I
know them better than they
know themselves I bask in
their adoration.

They think I know what
women want and I should
tell Freud
But do I know myself or anything?

# Summertime

Last night Leontyne Price
sang "Summertime"
in fire red dress
iridescent
arms outstretched
in benediction

I remember
summer times
Sunset Park
boy hood backyard
watching fire flies
phosphorescent
semaphores
in the dark
I played at war
Caught fire flies
with cupped hands
imprisoned in
empty Ovaltine
cans

and strawberry
jam jars
luminescent
beacons

Fireflies
Were my
imaginary
Armada
Zeros and
Messerschmidts
Dive bombers
Hornets and
Spitfires
Flaming
Incandescent

Last night
Leontyne Price
Sang  summertime
arms outstretched
fingers pointing
to the sky
While missile
Streaked over Tel Aviv
flashed
and died

# Equinox

the clock changes
the swallows fly north
they know when to leave
and where to go
they are programmed
while we flounder
aimlessly

we need to let
our garden grow

# Death

Death shall have no dominion
Dylan said
life is in the living's court
the heart is on fire
love and desire
needing
wanting
being
up and doing
like McDougall's
animals
we celebrate our senses
sight and smell
listening as well

we laugh at the grim reaper
and go about our way

# Eye

can an eye
make its self
can it evolve
incremental changes
natural selection
or does that defy
explanation.
the eye of the bitterly
or the eye of you and I
evolution
or intelligent design
Darwin
or only God
can make an eye
so we can see

# A Picture at The Prado

Fiery Night, Regulus light pierces Leo's sky
On earth leaves rustle. A lion roars,
Teeth gape from open jaws.

David's son minds his father's flock.
White headed rams and ewes.  We watch in horror.

Do we dare to tame the beast?
Do we rather run and hide?
A story is a tale, one as good as any other.
If it works, no matter

Where is truth? God knows.
But is God dead?
That puts de cart before the hearse the darkie said
God a she, God a 'mere' God is philosophy
Is that the point?
Who cares about the answer?

Philosophy is edified or dead,
Both or neither?  Deconstructed

There is truth but who knows it?
Philosophers perhaps not dead.

Embedded.

# Turtle

the word sits
on the flat back
of a turtle
and the turtle
sits on the flat back
of another turtle
it is turtles
all the way down
infinite regress
beginning
no ending
paradox
mystery
infinity
a story
without
an end
our world

# On The Run

from place to place
restless
exile
always looking for a home
a place to stop
place to rest
they played the violin
because that was easy to carry
in the pale of settlement
first the czar
then the Germans
why were they chosen
they could have picked someone else
trauma our identity
survival
our necessity

# Synagogue

the synagogue is God's theater
and we are the players on God's stage
origination myths
creation myths
who we are
and where we came from
we are in charge of our life
what we do
who we love
who we please
who we display
anger is allowed
there is always a final reckoning

Sartre was wrong
there is an exit for all of us

# The Talmud

the Talmud says there is an eye above us that watches
an ear next to us that listens
and a book with blank pages in which everything will be written
down
we are not alone
we are part of a larger plan
but I do believe in free will
I.B. Singer said of course I believe in free will
I have no choice
punishment for wrong doing
is necessary
justified
but we can't depend on the divine
there is no heavenly  retribution
as evidenced by the Holocaust
courts are temporal
local
not divine
judgements are communal
responsibility is shared
by all of us

# Dreams

dreams at night are what we wish for
dreams during the day are what we hope for
the mind is like the heart
which never stops beating
the mind never stops thinking
struggles knowing the difference
between reality and illusion
certainty is elusive
if wishes were horses beggars would ride
the old man said

# Memory: My Life
(written in my head while watching Maidel,
my canine companion)

memory is mystery
my earliest memory
my sister's third birthday
I was a year and a half
under the dining room table
did I want more attention?
probably
five years old reading in the Yiddish forward about the death of
Sigmund Freud
seven years old walking to school on December 8 and hearing
about Pearl Harbor
1942 my father crying when he heard that his father my
grandfather had died
of natural causes before the holocaust
his two sisters and two nieces murdered in the holocaust of the
bullets
his cousin survived,
she said "I hid behind a rock and my parents didn't look back"
PS 164 cultural anthropology
if I were going
lonesome train on a lonesome track seven coaches painted black
Montauk, junior high school girl friends

two Joans one Ruth one Anita
progressive party convention
win with Wallace and Glenn Taylor
Polio Haverstraw
Dewey loses Truman wins
Hiroshima and Nagasaki
the atomic age opens
Erasmus Hall, Marty and Nancy Bennett and Stanley, Richard
and Arlene
Aaron Glassman
Hunter College U of C placement exam
Arlene came after horseback riding in Central Park
Richard Asofsky
The University of Chicago Ernie playing the piano
New York love at first sight
wedding at Garfeins
three children Stephen, Rebecca, and Tamar
all special
five dogs: Sheba, Jiggsy, Ginger, Winnie, and Maidel
McCarthy hearings "have you no shame?"
McCarthy bad, Donald worse
the age of the dictators
memory defines us
what we remember and what we forget
who we are and who we want to be
our purpose
people and places
memory is our personal Google
Siri
On command

# Anniversary Song

I am old, but healthy
my heart is strong
my limbs are limber
I do not have delusions of immortality
but I have wishes for longevity
I have won the lottery of life
I have a loving and beloved wife
three wonderful children
many good friends still with us
much time together
years months, weeks hours
treasure every pleasure
measure every moment
my anniversary song
hurrah, hurrah hurrah

www.ingramcontent.com/pod-product-compliance
Lightning Source LLC
Chambersburg PA
CBHW071021120626
46546CB00003B/1193